J. D. Wilson is a 27-year-ol
blind and uses a wheelchair,
age of 10 to help her cope wi , something she
has continued to do ever since.

To my mum; I'd not be the strong independent woman I am today without you. Love you forever and always, and this is dedicated to you.

J D Wilson

WHERE IT ALL BEGAN: MY STORY SO FAR AND MORE, WITH A TWIST

AUSTIN MACAULEY PUBLISHERS
LONDON · CAMBRIDGE · NEW YORK · SHARJAH

Copyright © J D Wilson 2025

The right of J D Wilson to be identified as author of this work has been asserted by the author in accordance with sections 77 and 78 of the Copyright, Designs and Patents Act 1988.

All rights reserved. No part of this publication may be reproduced, stored in a retrieval system, or transmitted in any form or by any means, electronic, mechanical, photocopying, recording, or otherwise, without the prior permission of the publishers.

Any person who commits any unauthorised act in relation to this publication may be liable to criminal prosecution and civil claims for damages.

A CIP catalogue record for this title is available from the British Library.

ISBN 9781035870097 (Paperback)
ISBN 9781035870103 (ePub e-book)

www.austinmacauley.com

First Published 2025
Austin Macauley Publishers Ltd®
1 Canada Square
Canary Wharf
London
E14 5AA

I would like to acknowledge Austin Macauley Publishers for their help in getting this book published. I couldn't have done this without them.

Birth to Brain Surgery

27 September 1996, my life began
Three months later, cracks showed in the plans
I was supposed to be a picture of health
The next thing we knew, it all turned into hell
It was believed I had full sight
But then realisation struck, I could only see light
The next few months went by in a haze
In the blink of an eye, we had lost the healthy days
At five months old, it was a fight for my life
My brain was drowning and I had to go under the knife
They opened my head up and looked at my brain
The thing saving my life was a VP shunt drain
The surgery was over and my life was saved
Thanks to the surgeons, I'm not in my grave

Blindness and Me

Blurred images, nothing is clear
Light and dark is all that appears
In the dark of night, all I see is black
No glasses or treatment can bring my sight back
Doctors have tried to help me see
Nonetheless, there's no hope for me
Eyes are fine but nerves are shot
The sensory team forced braille on me as a tot
So hard to accept at first
Anger and frustration ready to burst
Nothing can be done, this is my life
Didn't think I could go on, I'm glad I wasn't right
My life is better now and my sight doesn't hold me back
Enough wishing I could see, I'm fine with seeing black

Cruel School

I cry myself to sleep after another day at school
Reliving every awful moment of the bullies who are so cruel
Unable to fight back
Every day, a flashback
Living in pure torture
School, arguing with Mum, who won't help her daughter
Calling names, beating, pushing, and punching
Hell on earth, my spirit crumbling
Only one thing can save me now
Only one person can break me out
Leave this school, leave this torture
The next school might be better
Her spirit is already broken; they won't be able to get her
It took ten years for the bullying to stop
It was only over after the school was dropped
Ten years of torture and yet it still lingers
It creeps into her head whenever she slumbers
Ten years on and she's mostly healed
She only got better once she stopped keeping her lips sealed

Living with Gran

Life was a mess, Mum was ill, and I was stressed
I couldn't help my mum get better
Violent relationships, she wasn't holding well together
It all came to a dramatic head
No choice but to leave
"Get well soon," I said
With a heavy heart and feeling torn
I packed my bags and left feeling forlorn
To my grandma's I went
Head hung low
"Grandma," I said, "can I stay?"
Relieved I had come to her, she said, "Okay."
All that was happening I explained
Now, many years later, things are healed and no longer strained

Disabled and Life Alone

Disability won't hold me back
It's moving day so time to pack
Setting out to live in a place of my own
Anxiety is at its highest but excitement also roams
Breaking into a new life
Learning who I am and what things I like
Everything is a challenge but I am prepared
Doing the best I can with the support of those who care
Asking for help when I need it is key
Not losing my independence or my identity
Disability is a part but it isn't all of me
Life is for living and I won't be stopped from feeling free
I love living alone but it can be lonely too
For a lot of the time, I'm void of company and it's hard for me to come to you
Every day is a challenge but it's a challenge I'm ready to face
All my life I've had barriers to overcome but I've smashed through them with haste
Love is the key to being happy
Or fighting for what's right and what you believe in
Nothing is impossible, it is just more challenging sometimes
Everything is possible, you can do it if you put your mind to it, if you want it bad enough you'll find a way

Destroyed by Him

Dating turned to torture within a matter of months and there was no escape
Every day a putdown, an insult, a new bruise or worse
Staying in bed for hours, not for sleep and not by choice
Too far away from family to ask for help, trapped with only him
Regret flooded me from ever moving there
Only regret was no use and neither were tears
Yes, I was trapped
Everyone back home thought I was fine
Didn't dare tell them how bad things were, wasn't worth the beating he'd give if he found out
Banned from speaking to loved ones, I did in secret but I couldn't be honest
You wondered why I didn't just leave
He kept me trapped, had people make sure I stayed and above all, I was paralysed by fear
If I left, what would he do, would he come after me?
My hell lasted eight months and by then, I was too destroyed to care what would happen if I ran
So I just ran until I was heading to my family back home and until I was finally free

My Daughter

The best day of my life finally arrived
My beautiful baby girl was born and changed my life
Light brown skin, brown eyes and a smile that made you melt
There are no words special enough to explain how happy I felt
It was the best day of my life and every day I smiled
The one thing I thought I couldn't have and now I was the mother to my child
Every day was a blessing watching her learn and grow
She filled me with such pride and love and I loved her with all my heart

Two years old and things would change
A new carer would cause me pain
She played on my weaknesses for her own gain
She'd gradually break me down into a broken girl
Manipulating me and taking away my world
She'd say I was too ill to look after my baby
She'd take her away and call me crazy

The worst day of my life was October 2019, the nursery called and my baby was in pain
She had bruises on her body and told them someone had caused this pain
Social workers were called and came to visit
It was concluded that it was the carer who did it

With a heavy heart and many, many tears
I made a tough choice that would haunt me for years
The next day, it came to an end
My daughter was taken and I'd not see her again
I was accused of causing her pain
It was later resolved that I wasn't to blame
I tried to get her back into my care
I wasn't successful and it was too painful to bear
I miss my daughter with all my heart
Every day without her tears me apart
I love her more than I can put into words
I wish to hold her in my arms
I wish I could've saved her from harm
I know I wasn't to blame but still feel guilty
There's a hole in my heart where my daughter should be and I don't think it's possible to rebuild me
I hate that carer and what she's done
But I refuse to be destroyed by this one
She isn't worth my energy or time but I wish she hadn't got away with this crime
Sometimes I feel like my life is cursed
But one thing is for sure, that carer is the worst

Pain Is All I Know

Pain affects me every day
From morning till night, it won't go away
I try to get through it but it is so hard
Nothing makes it better
I am emotionally scarred
Some people would give up and cry all-day
As much as I want to do this, it won't take the pain away
Living with EDS is a challenge for sure
Living in constant pain is a lot to endure
I don't know any different so I just battle on
Keep fighting the battles and try to stay strong
No one will understand what it's like to be me
Only I know how I feel physically and emotionally
Wish my pain would disappear so I can live my life free

You Can Fly

You can fly
Over the highest mountains
Up above those fluffy clouds
Conquering those challenges that life throws your way
Among the darkness, there is light
Nothing is too tough
For you to achieve
Live, laugh, love
You can thrive and you can fly as long as you believe

And now, some of my best work and my emotions in poem form.

Life Has a Reason

Every battle is for a reason
For the strongest people are the toughest barriers
You have a future
You are worth it
You have a reason
You don't have to be perfect
It may get dark
It may get hard
Just keep fighting
Don't let haters tear you apart

I won't be broken
I will be brave
I will not give up
I will not be ashamed
My life is challenging
Life can be cruel
I'll keep on fighting
I will not fall

I am unique
I am blessed
I am worth it
And I will be missed
I have a golden heart
I have love to give
I am wanted
And I deserve to live

My Hero

In these 25 years, you made me smile
You made me laugh and made me cry
But as I've not said this in a while
I want to tell you why
I love you for a million reasons
Not all of them, I can say
Because there are so many special things about you
And we do not have all-day

You gave me life
You gave me love
You gave me strength
And I thank the gods above
That you are my mum
My hero, my friend
I am so lucky
On you, I can always depend
You pulled me through the darkest days
And you prayed all my pain away
I love you for everything you do
I am who I am because of you

When I was a kid, we found that I couldn't see
You never let that stop me from being who I wanted to be
You picked me up when I was down
You kept my feet firmly on the ground
We have a special bond

No one can take it
With you as my mum, I'll always make it
So to my mum, my hero, my best friend
Thank you for making me who I am
I am who I am because you loved me

Wish It, Want It, Achieve It

Wishing for the happy ever after
Hoping for joy and love
Enjoying the good times and the laughter
Never forgetting where you belong
You are strong and worth it
Only the battles you face will make you stronger
Understand you are beautiful and accept your inner fighter
Be who you are
Every person has a purpose
Live your life to the full
It's being who you are that makes you worth it
Everyone deserves to be loved
Victory is yours, you just have to believe
Everyone has the chance to change, the right to happiness and the right to be loved
You are destined for great things
Only when you believe
Utopia can be achieved

Pain Made Me Strong

Every scar, every bruise, every illness, every trauma is a part of me that I don't let you see
They are a part of my life journey and the strengthening parts of me
I'm strengthened by the fights I've faced
I'm a survivor because of these
Forever, I will own these wounds and face each blow I'm dealt
I will not break or give up but I'll let the pain be felt
The broken girl you once knew, the one who'd felt so broken
I am not that girl anymore; I take the badness as a token
A token to remind me I'm stronger now because of all this pain
I will stand tall and face it all and never feel ashamed

Smile Though It Hurts

Tears may be welling in your eyes
You must smile though you'd rather cry
Pain may be spreading through you like a fire
Keep on smiling even though you're tired

There are some battles you cannot see
You fight and fight begging to be free
There are some scars that are more than skin-deep
You feel so defeated that you want to just weep

Whatever battle you are facing
Whatever is setting your mind racing
The pain may last a while
But please, always try and smile

You'll never know

You always wish for more
Only because you can
Unless you're searching for something
Living far from this land
Living on another planet
Never to be seen
Everything you want, you can have in your dreams
Vibrant images of the best birthday ever
Even a racing car
Remember this, you have it all

Kept locked up in your heart
Nothing is impossible, you only have to dream
Of whatever your heart desires
Wishes can come true

Destroyed by Her

Don't ask me questions, I'll only tell you lies
Even when I tell the truth, it'll only make you cry
Stay away from your loved ones, it's only me you can trust
Tell you what, you can call me mum and let your real mum rust
Rid yourself of any freedom, I don't care how you feel
On your own, because you don't need them, that wound will never heal
You deserve to be unhappy but I'll pretend that I care
Enjoy a few laughs with you then destroy you by failing to care
Deep into depression, you shall go
But you mustn't let anyone know
You may be struggling but don't say a word
Help isn't coming, your cries won't be heard
Everyone else thinks you're fine
Removed from your life, they've got no clue you're lying

Say Goodbye

Sorry, this happened this way
All I want is for you to be safe
You stole my heart when you were first laid in my arms
Girl, I wish I'd done more to protect you from harm
Over and over, I replayed everything
Overthinking it all, but I can't control everything
Darling, I hope you're happy and safe
Being given the love and attention I wasn't allowed to pay
You are my life, my world, my baby girl
Every day I'm grateful I could bring you into this world
I won't say goodbye, it's see you for now
Because I love you to infinity and I know we'll meet again someday, somehow

Scream

Sometimes it hurts so bad I just want to scream
Can never get away from it, only in my dreams
Running is not an option, I just have to face it
Everything can get too much and nothing will erase it
All I ask is for a break from the pain
My screams can't be heard, it's just torture within my brain

The Zebra

The zebra of the family, the odd one out
The medical mystery, they're all wondering about
I may not be stripy but I'm definitely rare
Looking for answers to why I'm in too much pain to bear
A list longer than your arm of illnesses and drugs that make me rattle
I'm a fighter, a survivor and I won't lose this battle

Still Standing Strong

I may have battles that are hard to fight
I may not be able to see more than daylight
I may not be able to run and jump
But I have ambitions I don't plan to dump

I may have fears and pain of battle
I may not be capable of herding some cattle
I may be scared and struggling in pain
But I will not give in, I have a life to regain

I can study, I can read
I don't like to fail; I plan to succeed
I have grades to get and exams to pass
I will not be beaten, I'll have the last laugh
I will not give up even when I feel wrong
I will keep smiling and I will remain strong
I love a challenge and I have plenty of those to face
I'm a fighter and a survivor, that's what makes me ace

Don't Let Me Fall

Don't let me fall even though I'm falling
Open your eyes and see I need your help, I'm calling
Nothing hurts more than facing it all alone
Telling whoever will listen that you're scared but no one comes to the phone
Let yourself be heard and seen
Even when you just want to scream
Take it all in your stride
Maybe sometimes, you'll have to swallow your pride
End all your worries by letting somebody know
Fear is overwhelming and it's time to let it show
After the storm, there will be sun
Learn your worth and have some fun
Let the world know you look out for number one

Speak Up

Speak up when they're trying to keep you quiet
Put belief in yourself and don't try to hide it
Embrace your successes and don't shy away
Always find a reason to love yourself each day
Keep hope in your heart and don't let it go
Use every skill you have to help your confidence grow
Please don't let them silence you or me, remember to speak up and be free

See You There

See you there when I close my eyes
Every time I fall asleep, I see you there and cry
Everything I do to try to move on
You are still there in my head; you refuse to be gone
On my better days, you're a distant thought at the back of my mind
Unless I never sleep, you'll never be left behind
Torturing me in every dream
The hard thing is, it isn't just a dream
Every time I close my eyes, you are there and I want to cry
Remembering every bit of pain you caused
Endless nightmares but if only it was just a bad dream, but it's real

Fearless

From the day it first happened, I was expected to act fearless
Every smile I had to face to keep you clueless
After all this time, I need you now to hear this
Ready yourself for my words because I'm about to reveal this
Learn from me that it will hurt
Every time you trust but they decide to desert
Sadness may overtake you
Should this happen don't let it break you

Courage

Call on me if you need a friend
Open your heart, you don't have to pretend
Unleash the real you
Relax and be true
Answer your heart's question
Give room for progression
Everything is there for you, just find the courage to see it through

Without Her

Without her, my heart is hurting
In my mind, there's nothing that's certain
Trying to be the best I can be
Having the best intentions, I'll make you proud of me
One day, I'll see you again
Unique circumstances have caused this pain
To the end of time, you'll be my little girl
I hope someday, I can show you that you are my whole world
Even without you, I know you're still here
Reading my letters and counting down the years
Until we meet again
I love you, from Mummy Jay

Why Me?

Why do I have to struggle, to be in pain?
Have to curl under the covers when it decides to rain
Yes, I may smile but doesn't mean I'm okay
My condition is a challenge and can be a curse day-to-day
Even though I'm struggling, I'll still smile as I can't change the pain so why not smile through every trial

After

After you left
From my life
Time went by so slowly
Edges sharp as a knife
Reminds me I'm lonely but glad you're happy where you are
I'll miss you forever, my shining star

Falling

From here
And there
Lies everywhere
Love and loss
I can't move on
Nothing stopping me from falling
Give me a hand while I'm calling

The End, For Now

The story ends here but only in this book
I have so much left to achieve and things to learn or to look
Even though this book is ending, nothing in it was me pretending
Even though it was hard to write and can be very sad
Never felt ashamed to tell my story even though I was treated badly
Don't worry my poems won't end here, please be patient and a new book might appear

Thank you for reading my book of poems.
Great appreciation.

J D Wilson